Cactus Spirituality

Pater Hilarion

Cactus Spirituality

Pater Hilarion

Gary Young, CR

ISBN: 978-1-105-24642-5

Dedication

Trent Riney for his insights.
Keith Johnson for his investment.
Lee Thomason for his editing skill and computer proficiency.
This is their work too.

Editor's Note

This work is fiction. No actual events, no persons living, deceased or otherwise perceived, are referred to in this work. Enjoy Hilarion as I have, and take from this work the wisdom that it offers.

Lee Thomason
March, 2012

Preface

Hilarion was born on December 5th, 1985, during a workshop conducted by Madeleine L'Engle at Holy Cross Monastery overlooking the Hudson River. He came from my imagination, inspired by that wonderful author who had once again gathered her disciples to convey Truth by means of Story.

This work presumes that the reader is at least casually aware of monasteries, parables, Zen masters and dictionaries. The reader's lack is not presumed.

Gary Young, CR
March, 2012

FGY

I

An observer said this about Hilarion:

"He is thin because of life in the desert. He is happy to be lightweight. He is simply clothed; no luxury; no hair shirt. He has a hood for shelter, a tunic for modesty, sandals for safety. He takes care of his body."

II

When he returned from the Monastery of the Citadel, Hilarion started to pray before the Icon of Christ and the Lord spoke to him. “How did you find the monks of the Citadel, Hilarion?”

“I carry back with me a large bundle of complaining, my Lord.”

“I know,” Christ said.

“It was hell, but when every one of them is a complainer, my Lord, each thinks he's in Heaven.”

III

Inspired by the Gospel of John, Hilarion spoke to a gathering of abbots. The sermon was received with great awe. After the liturgy, the abbot of New Forest met Hilarion and bowed very profoundly.

"I do not want to be equated with the Sacred," Hilarion fumed.

"But I am bowing to the repository of the Word Who spoke through your homily," the other abbot rejoined.

Then Hilarion bowed to the other, saying, "I bow to the Spirit using you like a fire to purify my pride."

IV

One day when Hilarion was gathering herbs and greens along the emperor's highway, he encountered the local lunatic, who engaged him in a lengthy conversation. In the midst of their dialogue, it happened that the emperor and his retinue pranced by in a showy cavalcade. One of the younger nobles spied his monastic cousin, reined in his horse, and said, "If you were not preoccupied with such foolishness, you could chat with the emperor."

"And," the monk replied, "if you were not preoccupied with your foolishness, this friend of mine would share his wisdom with you too."

V

A brother returned from Rome with a new batch of regulations.

"I sent you to bring us the Pope's blessing," Hilarion groaned, "and you have returned with his headaches."

VI

A thunderous bishop sent a questionnaire to Hilarion: "My dear abbot, do you not believe that persistent heretics should be cast upon a red hot grill?"

Hilarion's reply was swift and simple: "My dear bishop, I believe that persistent heretics should be cast upon a red hot grill after their execution – but only if they are poultry."

VII

Once Lucifer himself appeared to Hilarion and said, "If you will just acknowledge that I have great powers, I will send you 400 novices."

Hilarion wrinkled his lips. Then he snorted. Then he said to himself, "I have my hands full with four novices now. What would I do with 400 of them?" Lucifer disappeared.

"When holy water isn't available," Hilarion told himself, "common sense will do."

VIII

A benefactor came to Hilarion: "What do you need most of all for your monastery?"

The abbot was quick to answer: "Holy poverty!"

The benefactor was quite edified. But the brother-procurator had a headache for three days when he heard about that transaction.

IX

Hilarion's admonition to novices:

"Open your mind before you open your mouth."

X

"I see nothing wrong with charging visitors to tour our church," declared the assistant bursar during a meeting of the seniors.

"Your conscience is bothering me," Hilarion commented quietly.

XI

An elderly nun from the Monastery of the Repose sent a comfortable padding for his bed and Hilarion received it with great joy. So, one of the brothers questioned him:

"How can you set an example of mortification if you sleep on such a pleasant mattress?"

"When someone demonstrates such a generous love and concern," Hilarion responded, "I would be a wretch to disdain the gift."

That night the questioning monk found the comforter on his own pallet.

Do you think he slept on it?

XII

Brother Simon spoke to Hilarion about their small number of novices: "I fear for our security," he said. "Novices make an ample population possible."

Hilarion made the sign of the cross in the direction of the monastery. He spat then in disgust. Finally he spoke. "David, son of Jesse, rejoiced in the numbers of Israelites and God wiped the census tally clean. For our sake, stop counting."

XIII

A young rabbi took shelter from a storm at the monastery. Hilarion greeted him with an embrace, calling him his elder brother.

XIV

A self-righteous cleric arrived at the monastery with news of the death of a notorious Roman actress, whose reputation was far from savory.

"God knows what killed her," the cleric sniffed. "What can one expect from that type, who was nothing but a public display?"

"I would expect a good show from an actress, but only God knows what I can expect from hypocrites," said a sad voice belonging to Hilarion.

XV

Hilarion said this:

"Scandals are only the shadows of contrast which provide the background for the purity and beauty of faith and holiness."

XVI

The juniors asked Hilarion to speak about distractions during prayer. As usual, he was brief but helpful.

"Ants and flies invade every picnic. So, we must learn not to sit near ant hills or their trails. And waving extra blessings will chase the flies. And remember," Hilarion continued, "too many sweets invite these pests. Enjoy prayer even when the distractions are part of it. Anyway, what's a picnic without little visitors?"

XVII

Hilarion's monks never tried to milk his emotions. They knew that his sympathy was sure but solid. Hypochondriacs feared his comments, as did the morose. He knew that his sick monks were indeed ill and that is why he cared for them so solicitously.

All of the older brethren recalled a sarcasm of his: "Some people go to their graves before they die. Bad enough! But then they expect others to weep over them."

XVIII

Hilarion was the envy of other abbots, who presumed that diet and discipline were responsible for a healthy monastery like Hilarion's.

XIX

A discouraged visitor came to Hilarion and asked if monasticism assured earthly peace.

"The road never overtakes the horizon," the abbot stated. "But," he added, "The journey is as important as the destination."

XX

Two of the younger brothers approached Hilarion one day while he was taking his turn at milking. They had a bone to pick.

"Why," the first of them asked, "is Brother Telemachus the usual brother you send into the city on your errands? Such preference will spoil him." The other continued, "Shouldn't we take turns?"

Hilarion did not look up from the milk pail. But he answered. "Telemachus needs to know he can still fly, Brothers. He's a raven. On the other hand, you are his trees, rooted and strong. He needs you here, when he comes home to roost. He cannot be what you are.

"Now this nanny needs me and I need her. Peace be with you."

XXI

Brother Justin said to Hilarion during his direction, “I'm really not all that bad.”

Hilarion offered a question: “Justin, would you eat an apple with a worm in it?”

The youngster answered, “Well, yes, after I...uh....” The novice realized where the dialogue was going, especially when the abbot slid his old pocket knife across the table at him.

XXII

Brother Jerome complained to his abbot that, after twenty-five years in the monastery, he was the same miserable wretch who came.

"Then leave!" Hilarion barked.

"No!" Jerome shouted. Then he added gently, "If it please you."

"Well," Hilarion drawled, "there must be hope for you because there was a time when you would not have added respect to your disagreement."

Jerome persisted: "Is that all I have to show after twenty-five years? A drop of manners in a barrel of bilge?"

"A drop of poison can kill. Your drop of concern is your antidote against discouragement. Will you accept such encouragement from an ancient oracle?"

"Are you humoring me, Father?" Jerome reacted without thinking first.

"No!" Hilarion barked again. "I've given you a drop of kindness. My daily ration. Get back to your vocation! Twenty-five years is nothing to eternity! Results! Everyone wants results!"

XXIII

"Humility," Hilarion reflected, "is the ability to look forward to transformation in Christ, while keeping a spy's eye on the old self."

XXIV

A brother once remarked that common prayer at the monastery was too repetitive. "Perhaps," he suggested, "we need more spontaneity."

"Hmmm," mused Hilarion openly, "I wouldn't want my heart to function apart from repetition."

XXV

Brother Absalom came up to the abbot and said, "Brother Vitalis has visitors again. That interaction destroys community, in my opinion."

"In my opinion," Hilarion replied, "the great destroyer of community is jealousy."

XXVI

Hilarion overheard a pious visitor remark to another that monks have fled the world. Hilarion interrupted him and corrected him: "No, we have not left the world. We have stayed to protect it from those who have forgotten it was, at first, a beautiful garden. With our witness of praise and tillage and hospitality, we demonstrate our love for the world."

XXVII

At a gathering of abbots, a visiting prelate spoke to the assembly with great condescension. He had apparently forgotten that he was an invited guest because he related to the abbots as though he was the authority.

One of Hilarion's closest friends whispered to him: "Admit it, Hilarion, that man is a pompous ass."

"Tsk, tsk. A demon to test my charity has been knocking on the door of my soul. And you, my dear friend, have risen to open that door to let him enter."

XXVIII

A visitor came to the monastery who had known Hilarion since youth and had shared his unruly way of life. The abbot had not seen him since his conversion and was thrilled to see his old friend.

"I have not changed, Hilarion," the old man chimed.

"Neither have I," replied his affectionate friend. "But God has me and I can't have it my way."

XXIX

When he was asked about particular friendships, considered to be monastic bane, Hilarion said, "Most relationships are based on being trophy, toy, or teat.

"But," he went on, "if you have a friend not in those categories, let no mortal separate you."

XXX

Hilarion, casual about many details, insisted that the music of the liturgy be flawless. He stated regularly that music is the gift God permitted the angels to share with us when we left Eden.

Truly, Hilarion believed that the liturgy is Christ's restoration of paradise.

XXXI

Hilarion once told Aegidius that his life was a perpetual game of hide-and-seek. "But God always wins. Nevertheless we both enjoy the game."

XXXII

A novice asked Hilarion for a simple definition of the Incarnation.

Without hesitation, the abbot declared: “It is the unmistakable passionate presence of a loving God.”

XXXIII

When Brother Aegidius was dying, Hilarion found Brother Simplicius with the old man. Simplicius was writing several letters to departed relatives, friends, and confreres, which he asked the departing Aegidius to carry to Heaven. Hilarion stepped back from the deathbed and asked the infirmarian for some writing materials.

The nurse replied unctuously to the abbot's request, "How kind of you to reinforce the childish faith of Simplicius."

"Perhaps," replied the abbot. "But it is also the other way. Simplicius strengthens my faith. And besides that," he continued, "Aegidius has always been a great messenger."

XXXIV

Brother Baranek asked Hilarion about the strength of mortal fear.

"It is the sure treatment for Pride," Hilarion said. "No one who trembles can ever be tempted to play God."

XXXV

One summer night when Hilarion had just fallen asleep, he entered a fantastic dream. He saw himself before the throne of God bathed in a golden light. His cowl had become a purple cloak. His head was crowned with an olive wreath. His sunburn had been bleached. Breezes fanned his face.

He awoke and wiped off the sweat. "What a nightmare," Hilarion said to himself. Then he got on his knees and prayed: "Lord, never clothe me with riches. You are wealth enough."

XXXVI

Hilarion and Brother Joseph were urged to visit a new church edifice before they returned to the monastery following a synod. To their dismay, the sanctuary resembled a shop. Joseph counted five representations of Jesus and eleven of the Holy Mother. Hilarion could not count the angels. The altar seemed dwarfed. It was difficult for them to pray there. "Was the sanctuary hard on your eyes too?" asked Joseph.

"It was hard on my ears," mumbled Hilarion, "with the clashing of so many symbols."

XXXVII

The patriarch of Alexandria and his entourage went out of their way to pay their respects to Abbot Hilarion. When they arrived, the patriarch's chamberlain told Brother Simplicius to conduct his master immediately to Hilarion. Docile as ever, Simplicius took the stately patriarch and three of his group to a site near the monastery where the abbot and the novices were digging a trench for a new latrine.

While his trio gasped, the visiting prelate cried, “Reverend Father, what do you think you're doing?”

“I have taken inspiration from the pharaohs, Holiness, and I am preparing a monument for myself.”

XXXVIII

Once a critic confronted Hilarion with these words: "You are outdated!"

"Good," Hilarion followed. "I want to live in eternity."

XXXIX

A bureaucrat arrived from the Roman Curia and informed Hilarion that he should be aware of the new canons being promulgated. The messenger then left the abbot alone to read the list and took himself to the refectory.

He was not there thirty minutes when he insulted the cook, Brother Jerome, and the waiter, Brother Simplicius. Afterwards, he raged about the size of the guest room, which exceeded the abbot's quarters considerably. After that tizzy, he required a nap during vespers.

Later, when he asked the abbot what he thought of the new laws, Hilarion shrugged his shoulders before he inquired, "How have these laws improved your own spiritual life? Will our spirituality increase when we attach these canons to our rule?" Now Hilarion had no knowledge of the messenger's bad manners, so his questions were innocent.

That innocence drew tears from the bureaucrat, who declared that "The active love of Christ did not require canons or laws."

"Has your trip been in vain, then?" asked Hilarion.

"No, Father," the messenger replied, "for I should prefer to resign my office now and follow the rule of this monastery."

"As you choose," Hilarion sighed, "but now there will be new rules about robbing the Curia."

XL

A candidate told Hilarion that he had nothing to give to the monastery and that he expected nothing in return. The aspirant was immediately accepted because the abbot wanted nothing.

XLI

Brother Job came privately to Hilarion and poured out with tears a lifetime of anxieties and unhappiness.

"Who gave you your name?" Hilarion inquired.

"Your predecessor, Father," the miserable monk responded.

"Well, I'm changing it!" Hilarion declared. "You've had to live up to your name too many years. From today, you will be Jonah, for the mammoth love of God has swallowed you and your sea of tears and transported you to the other side of life, which is Joy."

XLII

Hilarion instructed the novice master: "Prepare your charges for the vow of Common Sense."

XLIII

Hilarion had enemies. Once, when he was in the city to see the bishop, a minor cleric, dressed like a potentate, let the abbot wait for two hours before conducting him to the bishop's presence.

When the two were alone, the bishop reddened. "He thought you were a beggar."

Hilarion dismissed that excuse. "Then he should have given me first consideration."

Now the bishop's face was scarlet.

XLIV

The emperor's niece arrived one day with a small retinue. Hilarion happened to be at the gate. "I have come to meet the holy man, Hilarion," she announced.

"Who told you that Hilarion is a holy man?" the abbot asked. "Have you seen proof of his holiness?"

"That is why I am here," the lady rejoined. "Is he here?"

"He should be at prayers," the unidentified monk told her, "but he is with a lovely woman at the present time."

The clueless woman sighed loudly but then she regained her usual composure. "If we hurry, we can make it to the Monastery of the Repose to see the holy nun Christina. Forget about the womanizer."

When the party was nothing but a cloud of dust, Hilarion mumbled to himself. "Tourists. Bah!"

XLV

When Hilarion first received his abbatial crozier, his staff of authority, he told the prior, "Put it in my stall at choir to remind me that absence does not betoken a shepherd." This abbot seldom travelled.

XLVI

A young monk, wanting to please his spiritual father, resolved never to waste time. So he devoted himself to more prayer and manual labor by skipping meals or leaving the common meal early.

One day, when he passed the guest quarters, Hilarion was entertaining himself with rich food and strong wine served by a hearty wench and laughing away the silence of monastic enclosure. When the master sobered, he found the shocked novice and shouted at him. "You deprived me of the joy of a son at my table, so I joined you in foolishness – only mine was more enjoyable."

XLVII

"I envy the peace in this sacred place," remarked a visitor one evening after vespers.

Hilarion smiled benignly, recalling how, at the noon meal, he had to pull Brother Linus, one of the cooks, from the recoiling body of Brother Sixtus, a new waiter, who had dropped a tureen of soup headed for the abbot's table.

"You don't realize how peaceful I am as we speak," Hilarion told the envious guest.

XLVIII

A monk, after a conversation with a pilgrim, approached Hilarion making a dither. “Father, I have just learned that you have enemies in Rome.”

“And have they hired you as an assassin?” the abbot asked. “You have just poured poison into my ears!”

Thus, another brother turned away from gossip.

XLIX

On a sad occasion, Hilarion went to the monastery of Greenfields to visit the old abbot who was near death. The old man was wasted with dysentery and was constantly fouling himself because of his affliction. Because of his withered frame, he was also a victim of bedsores. The previous physical dignity of the former abbot had surrendered to a pitiable sight. Hilarion thought he saw the crucified Christ.

"My dear Brother," Hilarion inquired, "how do you manage to carry this cross?"

The dying man's response was the glory of Christianity: "Hilarion, I have been stripped of everything so that I may see my creator more clearly. All that I enjoyed were distractions – gifts from God, but distractions nevertheless. Now, I have the clear vision of the one who hands the good with the bad. That insight is the greatest gift God has given me."

After leaving the dying man's cell, Hilarion sang an alleluia, the loveliest melody he knew. Then he told his companions, "I thought that I would find a crucified man but I have seen the risen Christ, glorious in his wounds."

L

The biographer was sent back to the city because Hilarion said, "How can you write my life? I haven't started to live yet."

LI

On Ash Wednesday, Hilarion prayed: "Act, Lord! I am Pharaoh, afraid of being weak. I am Moses, afraid of being strong. Act, Lord."

LII

A scripture scholar came to the monastery at his own request to lecture. He had promised to deliver insight into Paul's Epistle to Philemon but, after twenty minutes, several of the generous monks had drifted into sleep. The scholar took no notice.

Later, Brother David remarked that the speaker's wisdom must have surpassed the intellectual abilities of the brethren.

"Oh, no!" Hilarion declared. "The dull are never truly intellectual. They're slavers!"

LIII

When he learned that his abbot was confined to bed, Brother Peter sped to Hilarion's cell and knelt beside him.

He emoted, "This illness can only be the will of God which visits you today, which will visit me tomorrow."

Hilarion rolled his eyes and pulled his hand from Peter. "Dearest Brother," he growled, "I am brought low by a hemorrhoid." (He repressed a metaphorical comparison.)

Nevertheless, Brother Peter departed with the wisdom of embarrassment.

LIV

"I want to be perfect," Juventus declared to the abbot.

"You will be perfect when you can liberate yourself from the phrase 'I want,'" Hilarion countered.

LV

A second cousin brought her toddler when she made her annual visit to Hilarion. "I adore him," she told the abbot, who saw that the child was being thoroughly spoiled.

"I see," said Hilarion. "And someday you will suffer from the misguided will of a cruel god whom you are creating."

LVI

A brother, chafed by his hair shirt, once chided Father Hilarion for never displaying penitential practices. Hilarion, chafed by this brother, remarked, "Some of my brothers are my hair shirts."

LVII

The abbot of Mount Michael visited Hilarion, "I question the humility of your brethren. You are not severe enough with them. You are not stern with them. They are not in awe of you. How can they learn humility?"

Hilarion replied, "Is it not humility to live with such a man as Hilarion and call him a spiritual father?"

LVIII

Once, when many of the monks were harrying the newest of the novices during meal times, Hilarion rose from his table and told the novice to exchange places with him. When one of the monks asked Hilarion why he did so, he explained, "I noted that many of you had the novice fetching water for you, answering calls at the door of the refectory, wiping your spills, and what have you. You were treating him like a servant and not someone asking to be your brother. Then I remembered the words of the scripture: 'The leaders among you must serve the needs of all.' So, I decided that my role of abbot had been superseded by the new brother and that he deserved my chair."

After that, the novice ate his bread in peace.

LIX

Hilarion was the last to bed and the first to rise every day. When Bishop Polycarp heard of the old abbot's long vigils of prayer he sent a message of caution: "Your bishop thinks you need more sleep." Polycarp had been a monk at Hilarion's monastery until his elevation, and he chuckled at the hidden message in Hilarion's reply: "Come and preach to us."

LX

What Hilarion taught:

"Why should the angels do all the rejoicing?"

LXI

One day when the brethren were engaged in the manual labor of the monastery, a young zealot came to Abbot Hilarion and told him that he had become inspired with the idea of competing in saintliness with the desert fathers of times past.

The abbot sighed and looked up from his basket-weaving. "I have a better idea," he smiled. "Compete with the saint you were when you woke this morning; that would be more beneficial and," he added, "you would have a better chance of success."

LXII

Hilarion liked to quote the great Augustine of Hippo when he greeted novices to the brotherhood: "*Da mihi amantem et sentit quod dico.*"

That is: "Give me one who loves and he knows of what I speak."

LXIII

One afternoon Brother Tiberius was beating the monastery's donkey. Hilarion sent Tiberius to the refectory for a late lunch. Then Hilarion took the beast to the manger and fed him. The abbot then wrapped his arm around the donkey's neck and whispered in his ear. "Tiberius would be mortified if he knew he was abusing my favorite member of the community. The most docile. The most gentle. The most loveable."

LXIV

During chapter of faults, two of the brethren proclaimed Simplicius for falling asleep during the choral office.

"With which psalm did he start to nod?" Abbot Hilarion asked the accusers. When they told Hilarion it was Psalm XXIII, he smiled.

"So, Simplicius, the assurance in those words reduced you to sleepiness and your brothers have proclaimed you. Now, I proclaim them for becoming distracted by you and by not closing their eyes and for not opening their hearts to the Lord's goodness. But God help you, Simplicius, if you ever start to snore."

LXV

One morning when Hilarion was visiting his sick brethren, he overheard the monastery's hypochondriac nagging the infirmarian. As soon as he left the area, Hilarion summoned the carpenter, the hebdomadary, and the regulator.

That afternoon Hilarion visited the hypochondriac who was patting his forehead with vinegar. "Brother," Hilarion asked, "do you hear the hammering on a coffin? Do you hear the requiem practice? Do you hear the tolling? Do you recognize these holy oils?"

"Good heavens," started the brother, "Who is dying? Is it the plague?" Hilarion shook his head.

"The stage is set for you, Brother," Hilarion said ponderously. "No man can have the ills you have and survive the day, so I have come to perform the final rites for you."

The monk fainted. The abbot sprinkled him with holy water. The monk revived. "Have you learned your lesson?" his abbot asked. "So that you do," he continued, "I'm giving you the infirmarian's post and I'm letting that saint rest for a long time."

LXVI

Once when the monks were eating the noon meal, the porter whispered to Hilarion, "Father Abbot, the son of Lord Eyal is here with his retinue and wishes to eat at your table. He has brought raisins, honeycakes, and fine foods to share I cannot name. He has other young men and, uh, certain women with him."

After Hilarion repeated the request to the community, a brother said, "Father, to share our refectory with such a crowd is an infraction of our vows. Can't you send them to the guest lodge?"

"Open the great door!" Hilarion said. "Love is the first vow."

www.ingramcontent.com/pod-product-compliance
Ingram Content Group UK Ltd.
Pitfield, Milton Keynes, MK11 3LW, UK
UKHW020218250726
13967UKWH00001B/72

9 781105 246425